CHAPTER 1

THE FRENCH & INDIAN WAR

British redcoats march into the **North American woods** many years before 1776. This **French and Indian War** is a fight to see which empire will control North America. Will it be the French and their American Indian friends or will it be the British and their American colonists? The leaders and lessons of this war will soon lead to another war in these woods . . .

HOW DID THE FRENCH & INDIAN WAR BEGIN?

ⓞNE DAY IN **1754** ON A FARM IN VIRGINIA'S APPALACHIAN MOUNTAINS...

≡SNAP≡ RUSTLE

oh No— **INDIAN ATTACK!**

Wha..?!

HOLD YOUR FIRE, SETTLER! I AM **GEORGE WASHINGTON.** CAN MY MEN CAMP HERE TONIGHT? WE ARE ON OUR WAY TO ATTACK THE FRENCH FORT DUQUESNE ON THE **OHIO RIVER.**

SAY "FORT DOO-KANE"

GOOD! THOSE FRENCH FUR TRADERS ARE RUNNING ALL OVER OUR OHIO VALLEY!! AND THEIR INDIAN FRIENDS ATTACK SETTLERS.

FORT FRONTENAC
ST. LAWRENCE RIVER
LAKE ONTARIO
French Canada
FORT DETROIT
FORT NIAGARA
LAKE ERIE
APPALACHIAN MOUNTAINS
NEW YORK
FORT Le BOEUF
PENNSYLVANIA
FORT DUQUESNE
PHILADELPHIA
OHIO RIVER
POTOMAC RIVER
MARYLAND
CHESAPEAKE BAY
DELAWARE
VIRGINIA
WILLIAMSBURG
BOYD '01

FOR A CENTURY, ENGLISH PEOPLE IN NORTH AMERICA HAVE BEEN FIGHTING SMALL BATTLES AGAINST THE FRENCH AND THEIR INDIAN FRIENDS. THE FRENCH ARE NOW BUILDING FORTS TO CONTROL THE OHIO.

MAY 28, 1754: IN WESTERN PENNSYLVANIA, WASHINGTON'S MEN SURPRISE A FEW FRENCH SOLDIERS.

MMM! FRENCH TOAST!

OF COURSE, YOU REALIZE THIS MEANS **WAR!!**

WASHINGTON IS 22 YEARS OLD, LEADING 180 MEN. HE PREPARES FOR A COUNTER-ATTACK BY BUILDING FORT NECESSITY IN GREAT MEADOWS, PENNSYLVANIA. ABOUT 1,000 FRENCH AND INDIANS FORCE HIS SURRENDER IN JULY.

THIS FIGHT IS THE UNOFFICIAL START TO A WORLD WAR BETWEEN FRANCE AND ENGLAND!!!

NEXT: **GEN. BRADDUCK!**

HOW DID WASHINGTON LEARN WARFARE?

IN **1755**, BRITAIN AND FRANCE ARE FIGHTING TO SEE WHO WILL CONTROL THE OHIO RIVER VALLEY. BRITAIN SENDS GENERAL EDWARD BRADDOCK TO THROW THE FRENCH OUT OF FORT DUQUESNE ON THE OHIO RIVER.

SIR, I MUST REPEAT MY CONCERN ABOUT THE ORDER OF THIS MARCH.

PIPE DOWN, **GEORGE WASHINGTON**! YOU VOLUNTEERED TO LEARN HOW TO BE A SOLDIER. SO OBSERVE HOW A **TRUE** ARMY'S NEAT, ORD—

SUDDENLY FRENCH AND INDIANS AMBUSH THE BRITISH REDCOATS!

RE-FORM! DO NOT PANIC, MEN! MOVE TO — ARRK

WHERE **ARE** THEY?! I CANNOT SEE THEM HIDING IN THE WOODS!!

THIS ATTACK ON JULY 18, 1755, KILLS OR WOUNDS ABOUT 1000 BRITISH TROOPS. BRADDOCK DIES.

GEORGE... YOU CAN SAY "I TOLD YOU SO."

I TOLD YOU SO.

FRENCH SOLDIERS CAPTURE BRADDOCK'S MASTER PLAN FOR THE WAR. THEY MOVE QUICKLY TO STOP AMERICAN COLONISTS FROM TAKING FRENCH FORTS IN NEW YORK.

WE'RE DOING FINE WITHOUT THE BRITISH REDCOATS. WHY SHOULD WE DEPEND ON THEM FOR PROTECTION?

BUT THE OFFICIAL FRENCH ARMY MAKES THE SAME MISTAKE BRADDOCK DID. THEY LINE UP IN THE OPEN AND GET CUT DOWN BY AMERICAN COLONISTS HIDING IN THE WOODS.

NEXT: **IT's THE PITTS**

BOYD '01

HOW DID BRITAIN WIN THE WAR?

THE BIGGEST BATTLE OF THE **FRENCH AND INDIAN** WAR HAPPENS IN QUEBEC, CANADA.

IF WE ARE GOING TO CONTROL NORTH AMERICA, WE MUST DRIVE THE FURRY FRENCH OUT OF THEIR CAPITAL CITY!

SHHH!

BRITISH GENERAL JAMES WOLFE AND HIS MEN SAIL PAST QUEBEC IN THE DARK IN SEPTEMBER **1759**.

AS OTHER BRITISH WARSHIPS FIRE ON QUEBEC TO ANNOY THE FRENCH...

ZUT ALORS!

...4,800 BRITISH REDCOATS SNEAK UP A NEARBY 180-FOOT CLIFF.

THE FRENCH GENERAL, THE MARQUIS DE MONTCALM, RUSHES 5,000 MEN ONTO "THE PLAINS OF ABRAHAM" TO DEFEND QUEBEC.

YOU WORRIED?

NON. I AM MONTCALM.

CALL IT!

BOYD '01

THE FRENCH CHARGE. BRITISH SOLDIERS WAIT UNTIL THE FRENCH ARE 40 YARDS AWAY, THEN FIRE GUNS THEY HAVE LOADED WITH TWO MUSKET BALLS. THE FRENCH ARMY IS DESTROYED IN 15 MINUTES.

THE BRITISH CAPTURE MONTREAL AND FORT DETROIT IN 1760. THE MAJOR FIGHTING OF THE FRENCH AND INDIAN WAR IS OVER. **BRITAIN HAS WON!**

N.A.

... OR **HAS** IT? NEXT!

CHAPTER 2

THE BOSTON TEA PARTY

The **American colonists** who complain the loudest about the **new British taxes** are from **Boston, Massachusetts**. These proud Puritans and patriots demand "**No Taxation Without Representation**" – and they are willing to take their argument to the violent streets if they must!

WHAT WAS THE BOSTON MASSACRE?

OUR WARS

THE STORY OF AMERICA IS ABOUT MANY PEOPLE FROM MANY PLACES. EVEN IN COLONIAL DAYS, WHITES, BLACKS, AND NATIVE AMERICANS LIVE SIDE BY SIDE. IN THE **AMERICAN REVOLUTION**, BLACKS AND WHITES FIGHT SIDE BY SIDE TOO.

IN **1770**, MORE THAN 400,000 BLACK SLAVES LIVE IN BRITAIN'S 13 AMERICAN COLONIES. (THE TOTAL COLONIAL POPULATION IS 2.1 MILLION.)

CLANG CLANG

CRISPUS ATTUCKS IS AN ESCAPED SLAVE LIVING IN MASSACHUSETTS.

THE ALARM!! SOMEONE MUST BE FIGHTING WITH THE BRITISH REDCOATS AGAIN! TROUBLE!!

ATTUCKS AND OTHER COLONISTS RUSH TO THE CUSTOMSHOUSE THE NIGHT OF MARCH 5, 1770

GET OUT OF **OUR** CITY!

STOP STEALING OUR JOBS!

LOBSTERBACKS!

KPOP

UNION

ATTUCKS AND FOUR OTHERS DIE WHEN THE BRITISH SOLDIERS FIRE. COLONISTS CALL THIS **"THE BOSTON MASSACRE."** IT IS AN EVENT THAT LEADS TO THE AMERICAN REVOLUTION.

NEXT: **Tea Birds**

WHY WERE COLONISTS SWEET ON TEA?

COME WITH ME, SAMUEL! WE'RE GOING TO **BOSTON**.

COOL. WILL WE SEE THE DUCKS??

NO, BUT WE MAY GET WET!

LET ME GET A DRINK BEFORE WE START. I'M THIRSTY.

2 SHILLINGS

YOW! THIS ISN'T ICE TEA! IT'S HOT!!

STAR BUCKLES

QUITE RIGHT. IT'S FROM ASIA. THIS DRINK HAS BECOME POPULAR IN **COLONIAL AMERICA** — AND SO HAS THE POTTERY IT IS SERVED IN.

AMERICAN COLONISTS IMITATE WHAT IS FASHIONABLE IN **BRITAIN**. TEA HAS BEEN POPULAR THERE SINCE THE MID-1600s. WEALTHY PEOPLE HAVE AFTERNOON TEAS AND SERVE IT IN EXPENSIVE PORCELAIN MADE IN CHINA.

DO YOU LIKE OUR NEW CHINA WARE?

SMASHING!

IF ONLY I COULD BE LIKE MIKE...

WHAT'S THE BIG DEAL? HOW EXPENSIVE CAN A CUP BE?!

DEBT

I WILL GLADLY PAY THEM TUESDAY FOR A CUP OF TEA TODAY!

VERY EXPENSIVE!! IT'S GETTING SHIPPED HALFWAY AROUND THE WORLD IN CREAKY SAILING SHIPS. A LOT OF COLONISTS BUY CHINA WARE ON **CREDIT** — THE PROMISE THEY WILL PAY FOR IT LATER. THEY BUILD UP A LOT OF **DEBT** — MONEY THEY OWE.

NEXT: *The Tax Master*

BOYD '01

WHO PAID FOR THE FRENCH & INDIAN WAR?

1 ON 1756, BRITAIN SENDS MORE MEN TO THE **FRENCH AND INDIAN WAR.** THEY SPEND TO WIN. . .

IN 1763:

We Win

. . .AN EMPTY PIGGY BANK?!

I WILL GET **COLONISTS** TO PAY FOR THE WAR, SINCE WE HAVE BEEN PROTECTING THEM.

The Sugar Tax 1764
THIS IS THE FIRST TIME BRITAIN TAXES ALL 13 COLONIES TO RAISE MONEY DIRECTLY FOR THE CROWN.

WH-WHAT? BRITAIN HAS LEFT US ALONE FOR YEARS! WE HAVE OUR OWN POLITICAL ASSEMBLIES TO TAX US! YOU ARE MAKING THIS BRITISH TEA MIGHTY BITTER.

BOYD '0

THIS IS FUN! LET'S TRY ANOTHER TAX. . .

The Stamp Act 1765
NEWSPAPERS, LEGAL DEEDS AND EVEN PLAYING CARDS ARE TAXED. THIS IS THE FIRST BRITISH TAX ON GOODS THAT AMERICANS MAKE FOR THEMSELVES.

HEY! WE DO NOT GET TO SEND COLONISTS TO DEBATE THIS IN BRITAIN'S PARLIAMENT! **TAXATION WITHOUT REPRESENTATION!** WE REFUSE TO BUY ALL BRITISH GOODS.

OK. **OK!** WE TAKE BACK THE STAMP ACT. BUT JUST TO **PROVE** WE RULE, WE'LL TAX THESE.

Townshend Acts 1767
A TAX ON PAPER, PRINTERS' LEAD, GLASS AND TEA. THE MONEY WILL PAY THE SALARIES OF ROYAL OFFICIALS WORKING IN THE COLONIES.

BUT **WE** PAY SALARIES OF ROYAL OFFICIALS WORKING HERE! THAT GIVES US SOME POWER OVER THEM. NOW WE HAVE NO WAY TO PUNISH BAD OFFICIALS. ARE YOU TRYING TO ENSLAVE US?!!

FINE! WE WILL END ALL THE TAXES . . . EXCEPT THE ONE ON **TEA.**

NEXT: **T TIME**

WHO HAD A MONOPOLY ON TEA?

CHESTER AND FIFTH-GRADER SAMUEL ARE IN COLONIAL AMERICA.

WHAT'S WRONG WITH THAT GUY?

HE IS TRYING TO BREAK HIS CAFFEINE HABIT.

N-N-N-NON-IMPORTATION! MUST N-N-NOT DRINK TEA SHIPPED THROUGH BRITAIN.

"BOYCOTT"

THE 13 COLONIES ARE PROTESTING BRITISH TAXES ON TEA. NEW YORK CITY, WHICH IMPORTED 350,000 POUNDS OF TEA IN 1768, BUYS ONLY 147 POUNDS IN 1770.

HIS BOYCOTT DRAINS THE MONEY FROM THE EAST INDIA COMPANY (A COMPANY THAT SHIPS TEA FROM ASIA TO LONDON TO AMERICA).

BRITISH PRIME MINISTER LORD FREDERICK NORTH

Tea Act 1773

WE PASS A NEW LAW: ONLY YOU GUYS CAN SELL TEA TO AMERICA. THAT WILL BOOST YOUR SALES!

WE HAVE TOO MUCH UNSOLD TEA AND TOO LITTLE MONEY. WE'RE BROKE!

WRONG.

HEY! YOU ARE GIVING THEM A MONOPOLY! AND IF THIS WORKS, YOU'LL PROBABLY GIVE THEM CONTROL OVER ALL COLONIAL TRADE! YOU WILL PUT AMERICAN STOREKEEPERS OUT OF BUSINESS!!

COLONISTS THREATEN EAST INDIA AGENTS.

THREE SHIPS CARRY EAST INDIA TEA INTO BOSTON HARBOR IN 1773.

UNLOAD THAT TEA!

DON'T UNLOAD THAT TEA!

HMM. SOMETHING IS BREWING...

ROYAL GOVERNOR THOMAS HUTCHINSON

THE COLONISTS' COMPLAINTS ARE SILLY. BRITAIN CREATED COLONIES FOR TRADE AND PROFITS! AND NOW THESE HOOLIGANS WANT TO GOVERN THEMSELVES?? PFAW!

NEXT: PARTY

1765 STAMP ACT CRISIS | **1773** | **1776** DECLARATION OF INDEPENDENCE | **1787** U.S. CONSTITUTION

WHEN WAS THE BOSTON TEA PARTY?

ON DEC. 16, **1773**, ABOUT 7,000 COLONISTS MEET IN BOSTON, MASSACHUSETTS.

PATRIOT LEADER SAM ADAMS

John Hancock CHAIRMAN

WELL, ROTCH? TODAY IS THE DEADLINE. WILL THE ROYAL GOVERNOR GIVE YOU A PASS TO SAIL BACK TO BRITAIN? OR WILL HE SEIZE YOUR SHIP'S TEA CARGO FOR NOT PAYING THE HATED TAX ON IT?

I—I'M SORRY, JOHN HANCOCK. GOVERNOR HUTCHINSON WILL NOT LET THE TEA GO AWAY.

TEA STANDS FOR TYRANNY! THIS MEETING CAN DO NO MORE TO SAVE OUR COUNTRY!

WHO KNOWS HOW TEA MIXES WITH SALT WATER

THE CROWD RUSHES TO GRIFFIN'S WHARF. SOME COLONISTS DISGUISED AS INDIANS JOIN THE CROWD. INDIANS ARE A SYMBOL OF FREEDOM TO THE COLONISTS.

♪ Rally, Mohawks! Bring out your axes! And tell King George we'll pay no taxes! ♪

COLONISTS GO ONTO THREE SHIPS AND BEGIN DUMPING CHESTS OF TEA INTO BOSTON HARBOR.

IN FOUR HOURS, COLONISTS EMPTY ALL 342 CHESTS —ABOUT 10,000 POUNDS OF TEA.

THE TIDE IS LOW. THE TEA STARTS TO PILE UP. SOME COLONISTS SWEEP IT AWAY FROM THE DOCKS SO NO ONE WILL BE TEMPTED TO TAKE IT HOME AND DRINK IT LATER.

NO BRITISH SOLDIERS TRY TO STOP THE COLONISTS. THEY DON'T WANT ANY VIOLENCE. A BRITISH ADMIRAL EVEN WATCHES THE PARTY.

YOU BOYS HAD A FUN EVENING! BUT YOU WILL HAVE TO PAY THE FIDDLER YET!

COME OUT **HERE**, AND WE'LL SETTLE THE BILL IN TWO MINUTES!

NEXT: The N.C. Tea Party

12

DID MORE COLONIES THROW TEA PARTIES?

BRITAIN'S **KING GEORGE III** IS MAD THAT COLONISTS HAVE DESTROYED BRITISH **TEA** IN **BOSTON**, MASSACHUSETTS.

NO MORE SHIPPING!! THE BOSTON PORT IS **CLOSED** UNTIL THOSE REBELS **PAY** FOR EVERY LAST LEAF OF TEA!

RIDERS ESCAPE TO TELL OTHER COLONIES THE NEWS. PATRIOTS IN MANY COLONIES FORM **COMMITTEES OF CORRESPONDENCE** TO STAY IN TOUCH.

COLONISTS SNEAK SUPPLIES TO THE TRAPPED BOSTONIANS. TO PROTEST TAXES, THEY IMITATE BOSTON'S TEA PARTY:

PATRIOTS IN ANNAPOLIS, MARYLAND, FORCE A SHIPOWNER TO BURN HIS SHIP CARRYING TEA.

IN LYME, CONNECTICUT, A SALESMAN IS FORCED TO BURN HIS 100 POUNDS OF TEA.

IN EDENTON, NORTH CAROLINA, WOMEN DUMP TEA TO SHOW THEY WILL NOT BUY TEA FOR THEIR FAMILIES.

BUT THEY STILL HAVE LEMONADE, RIGHT?

AND IN NOVEMBER 1774 THOMAS NELSON AND OTHER VIRGINIANS BOARD A MERCHANT SHIP ANCHORED OFF YORKTOWN.

THESE TWO HALF-CHESTS WILL NEVER MAKE IT TO A STORE IN WILLIAMSBURG!!

THE COMMITTEES OF CORRESPONDENCE DECIDE TO MEET FACE-TO-FACE IN PHILADELPHIA, PENNSYLVANIA, IN **1774**.

HI! I'M Sam Adams

MEN OF THE **FIRST CONTINENTAL CONGRESS**, WE MUST UNITE! IF BRITAIN CAN ENSLAVE BOSTON, **NONE** OF YOU ARE SAFE.

THEY AGREE TO BOYCOTT ALL BRITISH GOODS. IN 1776 THEY AGREE TO DECLARE INDEPENDENCE AND FIGHT THE **AMERICAN REVOLUTION!!** END

CHAPTER 3

PAUL REVERE, RIDER

One of the bravest **Bostonians** is **Paul Revere**. His father came to Boston from France to start a shop for making things out of silver. Paul takes over the family business. But the patriotic fire in Boston pulls him from his shop and onto the trail of freedom. Revere becomes the rider, the spy, the messenger, the alarm, the warning bell of the American Revolution . . .

WHY DID BOSTONIANS FIGHT REDCOATS?

N 1754, PAUL REVERE'S DAD DIES. THE 19-YEAR-OLD REVERE TAKES OVER THE FAMILY SILVERSMITH BUSINESS. IN THE 1760s HE JOINS SEVERAL POLITICAL CLUBS IN BOSTON. ONE IS "THE LONG ROOM CLUB."

BOSTON MADE A LOT OF MONEY DURING THE **FRENCH AND INDIAN WAR.** SURE, SOME OF THE TRADE WAS ILLEGAL, BUT...

BRITAIN'S TIGHT CONTROL OF OUR TRADE IS HURTING US!

NOW THEIR **"STAMP ACT"** TO PAY FOR THE WAR MAKES US PAY TAXES ON NEWSPAPERS, CARDS, LEGAL BILLS...

"THE SONS OF LIBERTY" CLUB WRECKS THE HOUSE OF A ROYAL OFFICIAL TO PROTEST THE STAMPS.

LIBERTY! PROPERTY! And **NO STAMPS!**

BRITAIN TAKES AWAY THE STAMP ACT IN 1766.

BRITAIN CREATES **OTHER** TAXES: **"THE TOWNSHEND ACTS."** TO PREVENT MORE RIOTS, **KING GEORGE III** SENDS 600 SOLDIERS TO BOSTON IN 1768. BOSTONIANS HATE THESE **"REDCOATS."** ONE WINTER DAY IN **1770...**

The Bloody Massacre

FIVE COLONISTS DIE. REVERE DRAWS A PRO-COLONIST IMAGE OF THE FIGHT, WHICH HE CALLS **"THE BOSTON MASSACRE."**

THE BRITISH END MOST OF THE TOWNSHEND ACTS — EXCEPT ONE ON TEA. ON DEC. 16, **1773,** REVERE AND OTHERS DRESS AS INDIANS TO DUMP BRITISH TEA.

WE'RE HAVING A **BOSTON TEA PARTY!**

QUIET! WORK QUICKLY. IF THE BRITISH TROOPS CATCH US THEY COULD THROW US IN JAIL OR HANG US!

AND I COULD LOSE MY SILVERSMITH BUSINESS...

NEXT: rider on the storm

BOYD '02

HOW WELL DID PAUL REVERE RIDE?

BOSTON'S REBELS KNOW THAT OTHER COLONISTS MAY THINK "THE BOSTON TEA PARTY" WAS TOO DESTRUCTIVE. THEY SEND **PAUL REVERE** TO NEW YORK AND PHILADELPHIA TO EXPLAIN THE ATTACK.

IN DECEMBER, COLONIAL ROADS ARE BAD. IT TAKES A MAIL CARRIER 10 DAYS TO GO THE 300 MILES FROM BOSTON TO PHILADELPHIA. REVERE GETS TO PHILADELPHIA AND **BACK** IN 10 DAYS!!

KING GEORGE III ORDERS BOSTON HARBOR CLOSED UNTIL BOSTON PAYS FOR THE TEA. HE PASSES OTHER "**INTOLERABLE ACTS**" AND PUTS GENERAL THOMAS GAGE AND 3,000 TROOPS IN CHARGE OF THE CITY.

IN THE FALL OF **1774**, LEADERS FROM THE DIFFERENT COLONIES MEET FOR A **CONTINENTAL CONGRESS** IN PHILADELPHIA.

PAUL REVERE IS HERE WITH MORE NEWS FROM MASSACHUSETTS!

SUFFOLK COUNTY HAS DECLARED ITS INDEPENDENCE FROM THE BRITISH GOVERNMENT.

IN DECEMBER, PATRIOTS LEARN THAT GAGE WILL SEND SOLDIERS TO A PATRIOT FORT IN NEW HAMPSHIRE. REVERE RIDES!

CAREFUL! ICE!

HE GOES 60 MILES IN ONE DAY TO WARN PATRIOTS TO HIDE THE FORT'S GUNPOWDER. THIS SPOILS GAGE'S PLAN!

MANY FAMILIES LEAVE BOSTON. THEY FEAR THAT WAR IS COMING. REVERE STAYS TO SPY ON THE BRITISH.

IF WE TAKE THE REBELS' GUNS AND POWDER, THEY WILL QUIET DOWN.

BUT WE NEVER CATCH THEM. SOMEONE IS THEIR "STORM WARNING."

HMMF! IT'S PROBABLY THAT RASCAL REVERE.

REVERE IS CAUGHT SPYING NEAR "THE CASTLE," A BRITISH FORT IN BOSTON HARBOR. HE IS JAILED THERE FOR TWO DAYS. WHILE HE IS THERE, REDCOATS CAPTURE GUNPOWDER FROM SALEM, MASSACHUSETTS.

I WON'T LET THAT HAPPEN AGAIN! **NEXT TIME I WILL BE READY!!**

NEXT: *1 if by land 2 if by sea*

WHO SAW TWO LANTERNS IN BOSTON?

1. IN APRIL **1775**, PATRIOT LEADER **PAUL REVERE** KNOWS BRITISH SOLDIERS WILL SOON ATTACK ANOTHER MASSACHUSETTS TOWN.

THEY MAY TRY TO CAPTURE JOHN HANCOCK AND SAM ADAMS IN **LEXINGTON**.

IF YOU CANNOT GET THROUGH THE GUARDS IN BOSTON, YOU WILL NEED ANOTHER WAY TO WARN THEM. HOW ABOUT LANTERNS IN OLD NORTH CHURCH?

REVERE

ON THE NIGHT OF APRIL 18, THE REDCOATS MOVE ACROSS BOSTON HARBOR. REVERE AND TWO FRIENDS ALSO CROSS.

WE SAW THE TWO LIGHTS IN THE CHURCH TOWER—"TWO IF BY SEA!" WE HAVE A HORSEY READY FOR YOU, PAUL.

SHE'S A BROWN BEAUTY! LET'S RIDE!!

REVERE BEGINS HIS RIDE AT 11 P.M. THE MAIN ROAD TO LEXINGTON IS GUARDED.

HALT!

IN THE NAME OF THE KING!!

REVERE CROSSES A MUDDY FIELD. THE BRITISH HORSES CANNOT KEEP UP.

HE MUST TAKE A LONGER ROAD. HE REACHES LEXINGTON AN HOUR LATER.

UP! UP! THE REDCOATS ARE COMING!

STOP YOUR NOISE! HANCOCK IS SLEEPING.

NOISE?!! YOU'LL HAVE NOISE ENOUGH BEFORE LONG!! WAKE THEM!!

NEXT: Concord Grapeshot

WHO WINS LEXINGTON AND CONCORD?

Ⓐ FTER WARNING LEXINGTON, MASSACHUSETTS, ABOUT THE COMING REDCOATS, PAUL REVERE RIDES TOWARD CONCORD. HE IS JOINED BY WILLIAM DAWES (WHO HAS ALREADY WARNED TOWNS TO THE SOUTH) AND DR. SAMUEL PRESCOTT.

WAKE UP! THE REDCOATS ARE COMING!!

STOP!! IF YOU GO AN INCH FARTHER, YOU ARE DEAD MEN!

TAKE HIS HORSE!

PRESCOTT AND DAWES ESCAPE. REVERE IS CAPTURED!

Ⓛ ATER THAT NIGHT HE IS FREED. REVERE WALKS BACK TO LEXINGTON. PATRIOT LEADER **JOHN HANCOCK** GOES TO SAFETY BUT FORGETS HIS TRUNK OF SECRET PAPERS. REVERE HELPS HAUL THE TRUNK ACROSS LEXINGTON GREEN JUST AS PATRIOTS KNOWN AS "**MINUTEMEN**" BEGIN TO FIGHT WITH REDCOATS ON **APRIL 19, 1775**.

THANKS FOR WARNING US, REVERE! THOSE FEW MINUTES REALLY COUNTED!

THIS IS "THE SHOT HEARD ROUND THE WORLD."

PRESCOTT REACHES CONCORD AND GATHERS 500 COLONISTS. THEY ATTACK THE BRITISH WHEN THEY REACH NORTH BRIDGE OVER CONCORD RIVER.

REVERE SPENDS THE WAR COMMANDING CANNONS AND PRINTING NEW AMERICAN MONEY TO PAY FOR WAR SUPPLIES.

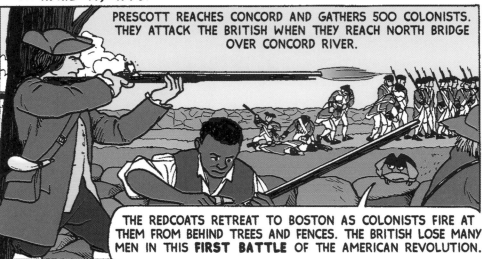

THE REDCOATS RETREAT TO BOSTON AS COLONISTS FIRE AT THEM FROM BEHIND TREES AND FENCES. THE BRITISH LOSE MANY MEN IN THIS **FIRST BATTLE** OF THE AMERICAN REVOLUTION.

AFTER THE WAR, HE MAKES 300 CHURCH BELLS AND THE COPPER BOTTOM FOR THE WARSHIP CONSTITUTION. HE DIES IN 1818. END

CHAPTER 4

A DECLARATION!

Even after "**The Shot Heard 'Round the World**," many American colonists do not want **total independence** from England. The steps toward independence come one at a time. And sometimes the ideas are pushed by what is happening on the battlefield. Will Americans finally get their **rights** inside the British government, or outside it?

WHO WAS THE 1ST CONTINENTAL CONGRESS?

AFTER DAYS OF TRAVELING, VIRGINIANS BETTY AND PEYTON RANDOLPH REACH PHILADELPHIA IN THE FALL OF 1774.

WHAT A BIG CITY! THERE MUST BE 25,000 PEOPLE!

WELCOME REVOLUTIONARY CONVENTION

AND 40 OR SO WILL MEET TO DEBATE OUR POLITICAL RIGHTS!

SEPT. 5 BEGINS THE FIRST CONTINENTAL CONGRESS. RANDOLPH IS UNANIMOUSLY ELECTED PRESIDENT OF THIS MEETING OF POWERFUL MEN FROM 12 COLONIES.*

HOW SHALL WE VOTE? WHICH COLONIES WILL HAVE A BIGGER SAY IN THIS?

JOHN ADAMS LOUD PATRIOT LEADER FROM MASSACHUSETTS

THE DIFFERENCES BETWEEN COLONIES SHOULD BE NO MORE! I AM NOT A "VIRGINIAN" BUT AN AMERICAN!

PATRICK HENRY VIRGINIA POLITICIAN

GEORGE WASHINGTON VIRGINIA MILITIA COLONEL

SAM ADAMS NEWSPAPER PUBLISHER. COUSIN TO JOHN ADAMS

*GEORGIA DID NOT ATTEND.

A GOOD START TO TALKS ABOUT HOW TO WIN OUR RIGHTS FROM ENGLAND!

LET US BE EQUAL THEN — ONE VOTE FOR EACH COLONY.

JOHN JAY NEW YORK LEADER

THE CONGRESS HAS TROUBLE AGREEING. FARMERS FIGHT WITH STORE OWNERS. BIG LANDOWNERS DISAGREE WITH SMALL LANDOWNERS. SUDDENLY...

PAUL REVERE! NEWS FROM MASSACHUSETTS??

SUFFOLK COUNTY HAS PROCLAIMED ITS INDEPENDENCE FROM ENGLISH GOVERNMENT!

INSPIRED BY SUFFOLK, THE CONGRESS CALLS FOR ALL COLONIES TO BOYCOTT (STOP BUYING) ENGLISH GOODS AND SERVICES. THEN THEY ADJOURN.

THIS BOYCOTT WILL MAKE ENGLAND RESPECT OUR RIGHTS! GOOD WORK FOR TWO MONTHS OF TALK, EH, MR. RANDOLPH?

HMMM

NEXT: FIRST FIGHTS

WHEN DID COLONISTS GET FIRED UP?

IN THE SPRING OF 1775, AMERICAN COLONISTS WONDER IF THEY SHOULD BREAK FROM BRITAIN. . .

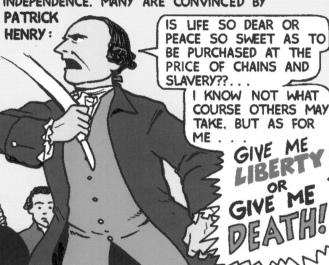

VIRGINIANS MEET IN MARCH TO DEBATE INDEPENDENCE. MANY ARE CONVINCED BY PATRICK HENRY:

IS LIFE SO DEAR OR PEACE SO SWEET AS TO BE PURCHASED AT THE PRICE OF CHAINS AND SLAVERY??. . .

I KNOW NOT WHAT COURSE OTHERS MAY TAKE, BUT AS FOR ME . . . GIVE ME **LIBERTY** OR GIVE ME **DEATH!**

BRITAIN PUNISHES BOSTON PATRIOTS WITH "**THE COERCIVE** (KO-ER-SIVE) **ACTS**." THE PORT IS CLOSED, TOWN MEETINGS ARE BANNED, AND MORE REDCOAT SOLDIERS ARE SENT THERE.

OUR SOLDIERS SHOULD CAPTURE ANY GUNS THE REBELS HAVE HIDDEN!

Lord North

ON **APRIL 19, 1775**, 700 REDCOATS SEARCH **LEXINGTON**, MASSACHUSETTS FOR GUNS. PATRIOT MINUTEMEN TRY TO STOP THEM.

A FREE BLACK (LEMUEL HAYNES) AND A SLAVE (PRINCE EASTERBROOKS) ARE ON LEXINGTON GREEN AMONG THE FARMERS. SOMEONE OPENS FIRE — THIS IS CALLED "**THE SHOT HEARD ROUND THE WORLD**."

NOW THE AMERICAN COLONISTS ARE AT WAR WITH BRITAIN!

THE "MINUTEMEN" KEEP THE REDCOATS FROM CROSSING NORTH BRIDGE AT **CONCORD**. AS THE REDCOATS RETREAT TO BOSTON, THE COLONISTS FIRE AT THEM FROM BEHIND TREES AND WALLS, KILLING 73 AND WOUNDING 74. FORTY-NINE COLONISTS ARE KILLED IN THIS FIRST DAY OF FIGHTING.

NEXT: BUNKER BEDS

WERE BLACK COLONISTS AT BREED'S HILL?

THE SECOND CONTINENTAL CONGRESS MEETS IN PHILADELPHIA IN MAY 1775. VIRGINIAN PEYTON RANDOLPH IS AGAIN ELECTED PRESIDENT.

MMMM, PEYTON HAS PUDDING!

I NOMINATE GEORGE WASHINGTON TO BE OUR COMMANDER-IN-CHIEF. HE CAN LEAD THE SOLDIERS FIGHTING BRITISH REDCOATS AROUND BOSTON.

THE REDCOATS RETREAT TO BOSTON. ABOUT 15,000 COLONISTS SURROUND THE TOWN.

WE HAVE WORD THE BRITISH WILL ATTACK US TOMORROW. DIG! YOUR LIVES DEPEND ON THE STRENGTH OF THIS DIRT WALL!! DIG!

SURE ENOUGH, THE BRITISH ATTACK BUNKER HILL AND BREED'S HILL NEAR BOSTON ON JUNE 17, 1775 – BEFORE WASHINGTON HAS ARRIVED! ONE OF THE LEADERS OF THE COLONISTS, WILLIAM PRESCOTT, SAYS:

STEADY! WE MUST MAKE OUR LITTLE AMMUNITION COUNT. DON'T FIRE UNTIL YOU SEE THE WHITES OF THEIR EYES!

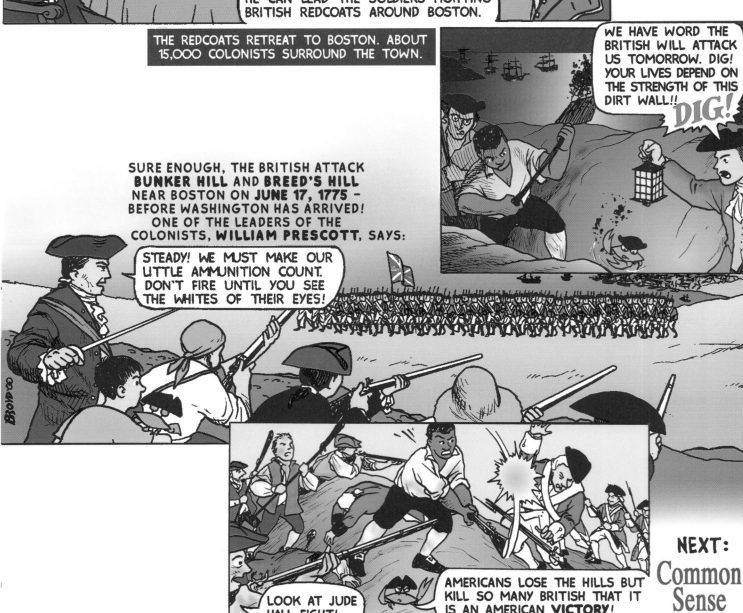

LOOK AT JUDE HALL FIGHT!

AMERICANS LOSE THE HILLS BUT KILL SO MANY BRITISH THAT IT IS AN AMERICAN VICTORY!

NEXT:
Common Sense

22

WHO WROTE AMERICA'S DECLARATION?

IT IS JULY 1775. AMERICANS ARE FIGHTING BRITISH SOLDIERS. . .

OH, THIS IS WHERE THEY WRITE THE DECLARATION OF INDEPENDENCE!

HOLD YOUR COLONIAL HORSES! AMERICANS ARE NOT READY TO TOTALLY BREAK FROM BRITAIN.

THOMAS JEFFERSON, READ US YOUR "DECLARATION OF THE CAUSES AND NECESSITIES OF TAKING UP ARMS."

WE WOULD RATHER DIE THAN LOSE OUR ENGLISH RIGHTS . . .

IN OCTOBER, CONGRESS MEMBER PEYTON RANDOLPH DIES DURING DINNER WITH JEFFERSON.

NOW WHO WILL BE THE FATHER OF OUR FIGHT?

IN JANUARY, 1776, THOMAS PAINE WRITES THE BOOK "COMMON SENSE." IT EXPLAINS WHY THE COLONIES SHOULD BREAK FROM BRITAIN.

COMMON SENSE ADDRESSED TO THE INHABITANTS OF AMERICA

REASON 143: DOUBLE RECESS TIME!

AMERICANS ARE FINALLY READY TO SEEK RIGHTS OUTSIDE OF BRITISH GOVERNMENT. IN APRIL, NORTH CAROLINA TELLS ITS CONGRESS DELEGATES TO VOTE FOR FREEDOM. IN MAY, VIRGINIA TELLS ITS DELEGATES TO ASK FOR A DECLARATION OF INDEPENDENCE. VIRGINIAN RICHARD HENRY LEE MAKES THE PROPOSAL JUNE 7.

MARYLAND NEW YORK GEORGIA VIRGINIA NORTH CAROLINA PENNSYLVANIA NEW JERSEY MASSACH

THESE UNITED COLONIES ARE FREE AND INDEPENDENT STATES!

CONGRESS ASKS JEFFERSON, BENJAMIN FRANKLIN, JOHN ADAMS, ROGER SHERMAN, AND ROBERT LIVINGSTON TO WRITE A ROUGH DRAFT.

YOU'VE ALREADY WRITTEN ABOUT THESE ISSUES!

WE'LL BE BACK LATER TO . . . AH, EDIT IT!

CHECKERS, ANYONE?

I HAVE WRITTEN SO MANY WORDS ARGUING FOR AMERICA'S RIGHTS.

NOW IT'S THE REAL DEAL. WHAT DO I SAY THIS TIME?

TOM MUST WRITE WELL ENOUGH TO CONVINCE OTHER NATIONS TO HELP THE COLONISTS FIGHT BRITAIN. LIVES ARE ON THE LINE!

NEXT: RIGHTS AND WRONGS

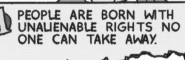